TRAVELS AND TRAILS

A Historical Tour Guide
to West Las Vegas and Montezuma, New Mexico

Travels and Trails

A Historical Tour Guide
to West Las Vegas and Montezuma, New Mexico

PATRICIA HALVERSON

SUNSTONE
PRESS

SANTA FE

Sunstone books may be purchased for educational, business, or sales promotional use.
For information please write: Special Markets Department, Sunstone Press,
P.O. Box 2321, Santa Fe, New Mexico 87504-2321.
Printed on acid-free paper
∞
eBook: 978-1-61139-678-2

Library of Congress Cataloging-in-Publication Data

Names: Halverson, Patricia, 1940- author.
Title: Travels and trails : a historical tour guide to West Las Vegas and
  Montezuma, New Mexico / Patricia Halverson.
Description: Santa Fe : Sunstone Press, [2022] | Includes bibliographical
  references. | Summary: "A tour guide of the original Las Vegas and
  Montezuma, New Mexico and the people who helped to develop the area"--
  Provided by publisher.
Identifiers: LCCN 2022011840 | ISBN 9781632933829 (paperback) | ISBN
  9781611396782 (epub)
Subjects: LCSH: Montezuma Castle (Montezuma, N.M.)--Tours. | Las Vegas
  (N.M.)--Tours.
Classification: LCC F804.L3 H35 2022 | DDC 978.955--dc23
LC record available at https://lccn.loc.gov/2022011840

WWW.SUNSTONEPRESS.COM
SUNSTONE PRESS / POST OFFICE BOX 2321 / SANTA FE, NM 87504-2321 /USA
(505) 988-4418 / FAX (505) 988-1025

DEDICATION

I dedicate this book to my dear husband who walked with me during the whole journey from the opening of Travels 'N' Trails Historical Tour Company, to stepping out to begin writing this book. He encouraged me, read and reread pages, held my hand and more. It is a reality due to his help and partnership.

CONTENTS

ACKNOWLEDGMENTS

For me it takes family and friends to write a book. I wish to thank my editor at Sunstone Press for accepting my manuscript and patiently working with me through the process, my mentor, Michael Olsen who read my old Travel 'N' Trail notes and gave encouragement, to our daughter, Leasa Martinez who was always at the ready to help with computer issues and proofread so many segments of the book, granddaughter, Hailey Botto who willingly contributed a drawing of a historical building and so many friends who lifted my spirits by basically saying, "go girl, go."

INTRODUCTION: EARLY DAYS

In the 15th century two separate papal bulls or pronouncements declared that Christians had the right to displace, and destroy indigenous, non-Christian people and claim their land. In various places across the world this has been upheld by courts of law into the 21st century. But in the 16th century, particularly in Europe it spurred the exploration race.

In the 1530s Cabeza de Baca, and Esteban, a Moorish slave, were part of an expedition exploring Florida. This expedition then headed west and was shipwrecked near Galveston, Texas. Four survived and were captured by Native Americans. When they escaped, they continued their search for a Spanish outpost. Esteban, especially, may have been enthralled by a Portuguese legend from 1150 AD when Moors captured Merida, Spain. According to the legend seven bishops and their congregations were amongst the Christians fleeing the city. The bishops and their flocks boarded seven ships and sailed to perhaps a beautiful island and established wealthy communities. The seed was planted and many were off to find these wealthy Cities of Gold.

Cabeza de Baca and Esteban finally reached the Spanish settlement near El Paso, Texas, but Francisco Vasquez de Coronado was chosen to lead the next expedition. Coronado was a handsome nobleman, a good leader, respected, and could finance the trip! Spain was on a trifold goal in its explorations, to gain lands for the crown, to gain converts for the cross, and to find gold. A Franciscan monk, Fray Marcos, accompanied the group and lure of the legend tainted all of them! By some Coronado's 1540 expedition is considered officially as the first Spanish exploration of New Mexico.

To protect the land from others claiming it, Spain and later Mexico needed their own people living on the land especially in the outer areas to act as a buffer zone for the more established communities. To encourage settlement of the newly acquired land, both the Spanish and later the Mexican governments granted large parcels of land to individuals or groups.

The family name "Cabeza de Baca" (C' de Baca) which means head of cow, was one of the early Spanish names in New Mexico. In 1212 the name was given to a Spanish boy who guided the Spanish Army through a pass which he had marked by the skull of a cow. The Cabeza de Baca family came to New Mexico perhaps as early as 1692 to 1696, but not later than 1803. Peña Blanco, New Mexico may have been their first location.

In 1815, the Luis Maria Cabeza de Baca family pulled up grass, threw stones into the four points of the compass and said together three times, "long live the king." Thus, they claimed the land at Ojo del Espiritu Santo which is not far from Albuquerque. Navajos made life hard at Ojo, so they resettled at San Miguel del Bado on the Pecos River, the principal town in the province north of Santa Fe. Luis Maria heard about the Gallinas River and on February 20, 1820 applied for a land grant. Despite controversy, Don Luis received the land grant. Officially the grant was known as *Las Vegas Grandes* or the Great Meadows. This land was really under the jurisdiction of San Miguel del Bado, southwest of Las Vegas, but C' de Baca went through Durango, Mexico, for permission.

On May 29, 1821 the land grant was finalized. The C'de Bacas built their ranch buildings near the Gallinas River and the village of Las Vegas began. The family was not aware of the vastness of his land grant, almost 500,000 acres. In 1826 the Rancho de Don Luis C'de Baca was the first house built on the present site of the city of Las Vegas. In 1854, Don Louis passed on but ten of his children were listed in the U.S. Court of Private Land Claims. In 1860, the U. S. recognized Don Luis and family to be the first settlers of Las Vegas. But other settlers to Las Vegas refused that and set 1835 as the founding of Las Vegas.

In 1833 a new group of about 29 people led by Don Juan Dios Maese applied directly to Santa Fe, New Mexico for a land grand. Due to changes in government in both Mexico and Spain they were given the very same land grant. It took the Cabeza de Bacas two years to unite and begin to fight for their land, but it was too late. The new land grant was call *Nuestra Señora de los Dolores de Las Vegas* and included some land owned in common.

In January of 1855 the United States had issued a notice to all land owners in New Mexico Territory to validate titles and claims at the land office. The Surveyor General, William Pelham was to sort through all these papers and certify ownership. He felt that both the Cabeza de Bacas and the Maese group of 29 people had legal right to claim the land. From 1887 to 1902 the U.S. courts worked on settling these complicated intricacies of the land grant. In 1902 a board was appointed to administer the Las Vegas land grant.

The United States Congress offered a compromise to the complicated problem by asking the C' de Baca heirs to forgo their claim to the Las Vegas grant and accept a like amount of land elsewhere. There were five different locations: Baca #1, six miles west of Los Alamos, Baca #2 about ten miles north of Tucumcari, Baca #3 three to six miles north of Nogales, Arizona, Baca #4 in Saguache County in the San Luis Valley in Colorado, and Baca #5 about thirty miles north of Prescott, Arizona. The Cabeza de Baca family granted several of these different plots of land to their lawyer for help in obtaining the entire replacement of their land.

The United States came on the New Mexico scene in 1846 and again the ownership of the land grant was questioned. Finally, Congress decided that the title should be to the Town of Las Vegas because some of this land was held in common by the group. Those who had small tracts awarded to them by the mayor (*alcalde*) of the town of Las Vegas, had the right to keep those lands, but the debate continued as to who owned the large portion.

It went to court and in 1887 Judge Elisha V. Long decided that the lands belonged to the confirmed owner of the grant, the Town of Las Vegas. Later in 1889 this was again decided by the court. The Secretary of Interior refused to recognize the order immediately, because the officials in that department still maintained that the land held in common had become public domain. It went through the courts again and finally by 1902 the confirmation of the decision of the local district court was made. But things were still complicated because the community on the east side of the river, since 1895 known as the City of East Las Vegas could not qualify as the Town of Las Vegas. But on the west side the community was not incorporated, so they could not qualify as the recipient. So, there was a push to have the west part of the community consolidate under the name of the Town of Las Vegas. There was also push to have the two join and the town in the court order be interpreted as referring to the entire community. The citizens on the west side of the river were suspicious of the aims of those on East side and decided that they would incorporate so that they could receive the grant under the name of the Town of Las Vegas.

In December of 1902 territorial supreme court Justice William J. Mills of Las Vegas appointed a board of seven trustees of the Town of Las Vegas for administration of the grant. Those trustees were: Jefferson Raynolds, Charles Ilfeld, E. V. Long, Eugenio Romero, F. H. Pierce, Felix Esquibel and Isidor Gallegos. From 1902 especially through the 1920s this board administered the area and sold much of the land to individuals and to land promoters, who resold it to people who would come to the area, and hopefully start farming projects.

People who received rights from either of these land grants settled near the current Plaza. When the second grant was awarded a surveyor was assigned to mark off strips of land approximately 100 yards wide up from the river. Thus, each family had access to water to irrigate their crops.

Las Vegas developed as two separate independent communities separated only by the small Gallinas River. This story will be explored during both the tours of Old Town (West Las Vegas) and New Town (East Las Vegas).

In the mid 1970s six Las Vegas historical districts with over 900 buildings were placed on the National Register of Historic Places. In 1977 Ellen Threinen published a document *Architecture and Preservation in Las Vegas: A Study of Six Historical Districts*. The Committee for Historical Preservation (CCHP) incorporated in 1978. CCHP and the city's Design Review Board led the way to help educate the community of the treasure they had in these old buildings. Thanks to their efforts preservation began.

THE TOUR

1
BRIDGE STREET AREA

Begin your tour going west on:

National Avenue at Grand Avenue or any intersection before National Avenue and 7th Streets.

This area is part of what was known as New Town, The City of Las Vegas, or East Las Vegas. In a few minutes you will be in what had been known as Old Town, the Town of Las Vegas, or West Las Vegas.

Park for a few minutes on National, just before 8th Street.

Imagine the area with no buildings, no trees. Imagine you have walked beside your freight wagon or ridden on a hard plank seat for months. You are dirty, hungry, probably sore, and ready for civilization.

Covered Wagon and Route of the Santa Fe Trail.
Courtesy Citizens Committee for Historic Preservation.

When this whole territory was still under Spanish rule trading with outsiders, especially that young country from the northeast, the United States, was forbidden. If traders were caught, they were taken deep into Mexico, jailed or perhaps maimed in some way and sent back as examples of what could happen. Spain was concerned that if trade flourished, the United States could come in and take over.

In 1821 Mexico declared its independence from Spain. The outlying areas of the New Mexico territory had often been ignored. Frequently their tools were decades behind what was being used in the United States. Mexico opened trade, the Santa Fe Trail developed and commerce flourished.

The Santa Fe Trail was not a single trail, but a broad swath as the animals of one wagon train would eat all the grass then the next train would go along side. This trail was a commercial trail, not a migratory trail. There was about as much traffic going back east as there was going west. It took approximately three months for a wagon train to make the trip from Saint Louis to Las Vegas. On the way they could encounter attacks from different tribes of Native Americans, drought, days without fresh supplies of water, heavy rains when wagons would get stuck in the mud, prairie fires, swarms of mosquitoes and more risks. However, if the merchants could arrive safely in Las Vegas they could reap large profits.

Goods going west on the trail included many manufactured goods, tools, shovels, scissors, razors straps, log chains, nails, pad locks, fabrics, sewing needles, sugar, women's fine hats and much more. The Eastern loads carried mostly furs, hides and Mexican silver.

Wagon trains left the Saint Louis area in April or May and started arriving in Las Vegas in June or July. The *Camino National* now known in Las Vegas as National Avenue, was the entrance area. Another drawing card, the Montezuma Hot Springs, were only six miles from the Rancho C'de Baca in Las Vegas. People started bringing their produce to the Gallinas River to sell to the Santa Fe Trail caravans instead of waiting for the caravans to come to San Miguel del Bado, which is about 30 miles southwest of Las Vegas. Scouts from Las Vegas sometimes would go north of town watching for the trains and race back announcing a train was on its way. Citizens would scurry to be ready with goats' milk, cheese and any available vegetables for the traders. Often the draft animals would be corralled in the space where the Exchange Hotel later stood.

Local citizens would quickly organize a *fandango* (a dance) and dinner. The captain, wagon masters, bullwhackers, and other travelers would enjoy a break from the 90-day trip on a hot trail. Many would take advantage of the hot springs at Montezuma. When they had accomplished all the trade they could in the area, they would either return to Missouri or continue to Santa Fe and on south until they traded all their goods.

In the 1820s–1830s as wagons approached Las Vegas, the traders probably were not impressed. From this view point looking down the hill they saw a small scattering of what looked like mud houses. They were not familiar with adobe building material blocks made with mud and straw, baked in the sun. These blocks provided excellent insulation, keeping buildings warm in cold weather and cool in warm weather. Then and today, adobe homes are common in New Mexico.

Old Town Plaza in its Early Days.
Courtesy Citizens Committee for Historic Preservation.

After you absorb that era jump ahead a few years to the 1890s. Just across the street is New Mexico Highlands University. General S. Kearny marched into Las Vegas and in 1846 claimed New Mexico for the United States. In the ensuing years the Territorial Government applied for statehood several times, but the U. S. refused. Some reasons being the lack of knowledge of English and general education.

In the late 1800s, the New Mexico Territorial legislature appropriated funds to establish two normal schools in the territory. Normal schools were dedicated to the preparation of teachers. One school was to be in Silver City, New Mexico and the other in Las Vegas. At that time the two communities of Las Vegas were antagonistic towards one another. If one side chose a site the other would object and vice a versa. They almost lost the right to have the school here. At the last moment both sides agreed on this site located between the two communities. The heart of West Las Vegas was the Plaza area and the heart of East Las Vegas was the railroad.

Springer Hall.
Courtesy Citizens Committee for Historic Preservation.

The school was officially authorized in 1893 and building began. In October 1898, the New Mexico Normal School at Las Vegas opened with

92 students. Classes began in the yet unfinished Springer Hall on the site of the current administration building. Frank Springer was influential in the development of the University and served as an early president of the board of regents. In 1899 enrollment increased to 195. In that same year due to the expansion of academic offerings, the name was changed to New Mexico Normal University. A model school also opened that year with grades one through eight. It was a student laboratory for training teachers; later a manual training school and kindergarten were added. In 1914 the school established a four-year program leading to a Bachelor of Arts degree, as we know it today. In 1941, with the addition of a wider liberal arts and science curriculum, the name was changed again to New Mexico Highlands University.

Early Class of Students at New Mexico Highland.
Courtesy Citizens Committee for Historic Preservation.

The University now has four sites away from the main campus in Las Vegas with total enrollment for the 2019–2020 academic year of about 2,800. The main campus enrollment was approximately 1,400. The federal government gave New Mexico Highland University a Hispanic Service Institution designation. To qualify for this designation at least

25% of the students must be Hispanic. New Mexico Highlands has over 50% Hispanic students and overall, about 70% of students are of non-white ethnic backgrounds. The University is working to become a Native American Service Institution as well. This requires 10% of the students to be Native American. As of 2021 8 to 9% are Native American.

The school is an important part of the Las Vegas community. It is one of the top employers, offers entertainment from sporting events to symphony concerts and much more in-between.

On the right, at the northwest corner of 8th and National, is the student union building, one of the latest additions to the campus. To the left is the welcome area with flags representing countries of the students. On the right next to the student union building is the library and across from it is the administration building. Next to the library is the science building. The campus includes several more blocks including dormitories, an auditorium, gymnasium, swimming pool and more. National Avenue offers the main pathway through campus.

Before you continue, step back to the 1800s. Picture the street with no buildings, cars or trees. As you drive on imagine a few adobe buildings gathered at the bottom of the hill. This would be the first trading settlement the wagon trains had seen in about three months. As you head down the hill towards West Las Vegas, step back to the 1800s.

Now continue on National Avenue and before you reach 12th Street pull over and stop.

Las Vegas now has over 900 buildings listed on the National Register of Historic Places. Looking down Bridge Street is a fine example of Western "boom architecture". National Avenue and Bridge Street provide a link between two towns with a blend of Victorian, Period Revival, and some adobe buildings. In the last half of the 19th century the economy of Las Vegas grew and building expanded. In the 1920s that economy started shrinking and continued to shrink until about the 1980s. In 1974 San Miguel County was one of the poorest counties in the state bordered by two that were poorer. During that time no one was interested in urban renewal as there seemed to be nothing to renew! Across the nation an interest in historical preservation began to grow. People started to discover a little gold mine in all these old vacant buildings. Dozens have been restored and of course, dozens are still waiting. Now tourism is an important part of the economy.

In 1531 sheep were already making a showing in the Southwest. Cortez brought them with him to Mexico in 1519 and by the mid to late 1800s sheep ranching was a big part of the economy. It was not unusual for herds of 200,000 sheep to be driven into Mexico and later into the gold rush area in California. By 1872 it was estimated that about 500,000 sheep were on ranches in San Miguel County. From the 1890s to 1902 wool brought in over a million dollars annually. In 1849 a herd of 10,000 sheep, when sheared, averaged four to five pounds of wool per sheep. In the late 1800s the wool was usually sold to mercantile businesses on consignment for 10 to 15 cents a pound. It was not unheard of for sheep ranchers to bury rocks in the sacks of wool. One way to minimize the misjudging of wool weight or shrinkage was to scour it clean. Ludeman Wool Company had a scouring plant with wooden flumes near the Gallinas River. Gross Kelley Mercantile had their own scouring plant and in 1901 scoured over 3,000,000 pounds. Wool growers usually readily agreed to the scouring, otherwise they had to pay for the grease and dirt to be shipped. The major mercantile companies all bought and sold wool.

Taichert Building. Courtesy of Hailey Botto.

On the southwest corner of National and 12th Street is a two-story brick building which became known as the Taichert Building. Four Taichert brothers were orphaned in a little village on the Prussia-Lithuania border in 1896. At age 14, Joe, the oldest one migrated to the United States to live with relatives and soon brought his brothers to join him. All the brothers learned tailoring. When Joe developed a spot on his lung he joined hundreds of others and came to New Mexico to recover. He regained his health, worked for a time at a mountain hotel outside of Las Vegas and become well acquainted with the mountains. He started trapping beaver and fox which he sold to the Charles Ilfeld Company. In 1912 two Taichert brothers bought this corner building and started their hide, fur and wool business which operated from 1912 to 1971.

Joe and his younger brother, Milton, started a haberdashery on Douglas Street which continued to be a mainstay in Las Vegas until 2006. Joe also started the JA Taichert Company which became one of the larger wholesalers in the southwest. Joe, chief businessman, also acted as banker and rescued mortgage debtors from foreclosure. The Taichert name was respected in the community.

The Taicherts also bought the building on 12th Street behind the business on National. This building housed the horses and trolley cars of the Las Vegas Street Rail Company which started in 1880. In 1881 there were four trolley cars. Each car made twenty round trips a day between East and West Las Vegas. Each animal worked three hours at a time, two times a day and averaged twenty-two miles a day. The fare was initially five cents a trip and later increased.

The building on the northwest corner of National Avenue and 12th Street was a livery stable and hack business. They boarded horses as well as hired out horses and carriages. "Hack" in those days referred to a horse used for riding or driving. In 1900 the City Directory listed M. E. Clay and W.A. Givens as owners. In 1908 the City Directory listed James Clay the owner and W. A. Givens as retired.

On National Avenue, just beyond the Taichert building is the Gallinas River. In English *gallinas* means "chicken." Legends say that the river was so small that a chicken could walk across without getting its feet wet. Perhaps so, but at times, the little Gallinas River can become a menacing raging flood. In the days of the first settlements, it provided water to cause the area to be called Las Vegas, which means the meadows. The first bridge, a wooden plank bridge was built in 1879. Before that time the wagons coming in from the Santa Fe Trail had to ford the river. This small river became the boundary between East and West Las Vegas. In 1886 a new iron bridge was built. This was the sight of many hangings. The present bridge was built in 1910.

Joseph G. Maloof was born in Lebanon in 1903 He migrated to the United States and married Frances. Their eldest son was born in Las Vegas, New Mexico in 1923. Here he started his brewery business, the forerunner of Coors beer. On the south side of the street buildings at 111-115 including the Kiva Theatre and 119-121 were Maloof buildings. Later Maloofs moved to Albuquerque and there expanded the distribution company and many other interests.

Cross the bridge.

Now National Avenue becomes Bridge Street.

Pull over where possible and park on Bridge Street.

You may like to get out and walk a bit and explore some of the interesting shops.

On the north side of the street at 116 Bridge Street take note of the Stern and Nahm building. It is one of six Victorian buildings on Bridge Street. The building dates to about 1882 when Isidor Stern and Sigmond Nahm formed a partnership and established their mercantile business in the building. They also acquired other businesses in Las Vegas.

An interesting side story is that Mrs. Nahm had some type of physical problems and consulted doctors across the country trying to find solutions, but to no avail. Someone told her that she might find relief in the hot springs at Karlsbad, Germany. Once in Karlsbad the doctors there told her that the only place in the world that they knew she could possibly receive a cure was a very small place known as Montezuma, New Mexico. It was only five miles from Las Vegas! You may want to drive a little farther west on Bridge Street or just enjoy the walk.

At 141-143 Bridge, where the El Rialto Restaurant now stands, was the location of the Shupp Carriage Factory. In the 1880s Las Vegas had several important businesses and factories with sales outside the area including a brick kiln, an iron foundry, flour mill and more. In 1884 Shupp's had orders for many carriages to different locations including one order of 44 buggies to Arizona. In the 1920s that building was replaced by the current Period Revival architecture building.

In 1877 a huge fire destroyed several major buildings on the south side of

Bridge Street. The original buildings were often put up very quickly with whatever material was available. Though the origin of the fire was never certified, it was assumed that a tossed cigarette butt in the packing area of a mercantile building ignited straw and wood. The destroyed buildings were then history.

Eugenio Romero made a large donation to help the West Las Vegas fire department get started. This building at 155 Bridge Street was built in 1909, but the *E. Romero Hose and Fire Company* in West Las Vegas and *Company Number One* in East Las Vegas were both established in 1881-1882. At first the fire departments had no horses to pull the fire wagons and depended upon the arrival of the first volunteer with horses. In 1902-1903 both fire departments bought horses. In 1916 both companies bought fire trucks. The *E. Romero Company* sold their horse teams to gypsies. At the first alarm those horses came on the run, dragging the gypsy tent with them!

Preservation of this building began in 2009 with the Main Street organization working hard to acquire several grants to restore the building and make it into a museum. In the process in 2012 Las Vegas received the "Community Preservation Award" from the State Historic Preservation Division and an award from The National Trust for Historic Preservation as one of the nation's ten favorite Main Street Projects.

The building at 157 Bridge, built in 1882 is known as the Hedgcock Building. Over the years it has had many uses such as dry goods store with different owners, a boot and shoe factory established by Charles Rathbun and then a man named Hedgcock bought it. Although he only had it for about five years the Hedgcock name stuck with the building. In 1939 the West Las Vegas town acquired the building for its Town Hall and other businesses have recycled through the space since then.

The last building on the south side of Bridge Street just before the Plaza was a bank built by Jefferson and Joshua Raynolds in 1880. Their first bank was located on the west side of the Plaza. The construction of this building is rather interesting as only the street side of the building was built with rubble (masonary mixed with fragments of rock or cement) based with ashlar (squared blocks of building stone); the rear sections of the bank were adobe.

Shortly after the completion of the building and after the bank was open for business, employees complained about an irregularity in the floor. Mr. Joshua Raynolds, the president, decided to stay late one night to try to discover the cause. He heard strange noises, called the police, and a would-be burglar was arrested. He had almost completed his tunnel from the building next door to the vault of the bank. The building is now the West Las Vegas School Administration building.

Across the street from the West Las Vegas Administration Building on the northeast corner of Bridge Street and the Plaza is the Plaza Drugstore. Miguel Romero had been a wagon master on the Santa Fe Trail. Miguel and his sons became prominent members of the business and political community of Las Vegas. One son, Benigno, opened the Plaza Drug Store in this location in 1884. He developed a concoction, *La Sanadora,* which was never approved by the Federal Food and Drug Administration yet claimed that it could perhaps cure most ailments! His brother, Secondino replaced the older building in 1919 with this present one.

The New Mexico Medical Society had its beginnings in Las Vegas and on January 7, 1882 physicians called the first meeting of the Medical Society. At first it was called the Las Vegas Medical Society and later New Mexico Medical Society. There were nine physicians present and Dr. Shout from Las Vegas was elected president. For many years they held meetings in the second floor offices of the Plaza Drug.

2
PLAZA AREA

Drive around the Plaza and find a place to park.

This portion of the tour showcases the Plaza. If the weather is nice take a walk around the park, maybe get an ice cream cone at the Plaza Drug, a snack at one of the other eating places on the Plaza, perhaps visit some of the shops or just take a seat on one of the park benches.

This is the site of the original settling of Las Vegas. People were drawn to the area because of the river and green meadows. Early settlers were granted strips of land from the river and soon small adobe buildings sprang up starting to form a circle not far from the river. Las Vegas had a strong community spirit and neighbors helped one another build their homes. The Plaza developed and became the focal point for traders.

On the southeast corner of the plaza stands a large building with faded letters above the door, *Navajo Parachute Factory*. Emanuel Rosenwald was born in Bavaria in 1838. He migrated to the United States, then spent some time in Virginia where he went to night school. He became a trader with Native Americans for a time and in 1862 he came to New Mexico on the Santa Fe Trail. He opened his business, Rosenwald Mercantile, here on the southeast side of the Plaza. In 1908 he replaced the adobe building with a new stone one. For 53 years he was a prominent force in the business life of Las Vegas. He stood for justice, honesty, law and order. He was respected, beloved for his charity and emulated by many. His son David followed in his footsteps.

In 1954 the Navajo Parachute Factory located in the building. At its peak it employed 325 people. Due to dwindling contracts it closed in 1970. Employees were paid by the piece. *Comadre y compadre* is a descriptive phrase. In this area it means the mother and father of your daughter-in law or son-in law. My *comadre*, a bright, creative, industrious woman worked in the Navajo Parachute factory for a time. Once she came home from work and told her husband, "If you could make a wedge (such and such) a size I could place it with the sewing machine pedal and I could sew faster." He did, she did and it worked! At one time a roller-skating rink occupied the building.

At 213 Plaza sits the Courtroom Building. Little is known about the building except that it was erected in 1882 and temporarily used as a courthouse until the county courthouse was completed in 1885. Then a variety of dry goods stores occupied the building off and on. In the late 1960s or early 1970s the lower part of the building was bricked in.

Three doors west of the Courthouse building, the Imperial Bar, sometimes known as the Victory Bar, was owned by a notorious character, Vicente Silva. Vicente was a handsome man, who operated a popular saloon, gambling house and dance hall. His obsession with wealth and power drew him into criminal activities. He joined forces with some of the unsavory men who frequented his bar and after hours they planned atrocious acts. They reigned terror in the area, but Silva seemed to maintain alibis. After Silva had one of his gang hung from the bridge, kidnapped his own daughter, had his brother-in-law killed and then killed his own wife, his gang drew the line and killed him!

The building on the southwest corner of the Plaza at 247 S. Plaza is an example of neoclassical revival architecture. The Miguel Romero family founded the Romero Mercantile Company in 1878. Under son Trinidad's leadership it became a leading wholesale distributing business in the Southwest. The earlier buildings suffered fires and this building was constructed between 1908 and 1913. Trinidad also built a thirty-two room mansion five miles southwest of Las Vegas. After many years of much hospitality the mansion was destroyed by fire. In 1911 Trinidad was appointed to become one of the first delegates to the U. S. Congress.

Across the street on the corner of West National, Plaza and South Pacific streets is the current site of the Las Vegas Police Department and the original location of the Exchange Hotel. The hotel was constructed in 1852, and burned in 1959. The part of the building facing West National is the only part of the original building to survive. The saloon and gambling area, also known as The Buffalo Hall, served as a meeting place for big ranchers, politicians, businessmen and more. It was not uncommon for a poker game to run for days. Meals and drinks would be delivered to the tables to prevent any interruption of the game! Later the hotel became a stop on the Butterfield Stage Coach Line. A large lot to the rear of building accommodated draft animals, wagons and carriages. The rooms of the hotel were perhaps not quite as popular as the public areas, especially by today's standards, the walls only went up half way.

In 1862 the Confederate Army marched up the Rio Grande and threatened to capture Santa Fe. Governor Henry Connelly retreated to Las Vegas, New Mexico and set up a temporary Territorial Capitol in the Exchange Hotel.

Take a few minutes to look at the Plaza. Imagine it as bare ground, with no trees, and very few buildings. It took decades for these historical buildings to arise. It brought a mixture of people from many backgrounds to make it happen. Growth was especially rapid after the first train arrived in 1879. Beginning in the mid 1860s Las Vegas was earning a reputation of being the most disorderly place in the territory. In the early 1880's things were chaotic and not at all peaceful, and at times violent crime became very high. A vigilante group formed and the *Las Vegas Optic* newspaper received this notice to be published in the paper:

> *To Murderers, Confidence Men, Thieves: The citizens of Las Vegas have tired of the robbery, murder, and other crimes, that have made this town a by-word in every civilized community. They have resolved to put a stop to crime, if in attaining that end they have to forget the law and resort to speedier justice than it will afford. All such characters are, therefore, notified that they must either leave this town or conform themselves to the requirement of law, or they will be summarily dealt with. The flow of blood MUST and SHALL be stopped in this community, and the good*

citizens of both Old and New Towns have determined to stop it, if they have to HANG by the strong arm of the law in this country.

(signed) VIGILANTES

Circa early 1879 the well on the Plaza was dug deeper and a windmill was erected. However, the well went dry and the windmill became the site of many vigilante hangings. The windmill was finally dismantled and the bridge became the hanging site. At one time the vigilantes stormed the jail in the wee hours of the morning and took five prisoners, one at a time to the bridge, prepared the prisoner for hanging and told them they either had 15 minutes to leave town and never return or be hung. All left the city and none were hung.

Incredulous as it seems, so many good things happened during this same time. At least one member of each family in Las Vegas could read. It possibly had the highest literacy ratio per capita in the territory. In 1881 all of the following took place:

Early 1881: Las Vegas Street Railway tracks were laid and horse drawn street cars operated on a regular basis. Electric street cars were operating by 1903.

March 5: E. Romero Hose and Fire Department was formed and the same year Company Number One formed in East Las Vegas.

March 11: First pipeline laid for the Las Vegas Gas Company. Stock sold for New Mexico Electric Light Company.

March 17: Stock sold for the first Telephone Company in New Mexico.

March 19: First telephone call in New Mexico (There was some concern in the community about this new-fangled technology. "Would it understand Spanish?")

In 1892 the *Las Vegas Optic* reported that Las Vegas was the most important city in the territory.

To continue your tour, give your attention to the building on the southwest corner of Plaza and West National Streets. In 1836, very soon after the settling of Las Vegas, members of the community built the first Our Lady of Sorrows Church on this site and expected every family to contribute to the effort. After a few years that building burned and John Dold opened a mercantile business in this building at 1805 West Plaza.

John and his brother Andres Dold came to Las Vegas shortly after the Civil War. They had mercantile businesses on opposite corners of the Plaza. John's building originally had a two-story portal with both first and second story openings. It was an elegant building. The Dold business closed and other businesses began locating at the site. In 1890 Ike Davis opened his long-lasting popular grocery store at the site.

The location of the Andres Dold building is uncertain, but for many years Andres was a prominent merchant, banker, retail merchant, owner and operator of wagon trains. He was also known as a shrewd businessman, not missing a trick!

About a block west on West National the current Our Lady of Sorrows was started in 1851 and completed in 1870, with church registers beginning in 1852. The stone came from a nearby quarry and the *vigas* (beams or rafters) came from the Rociada area north of Las Vegas.

Charles Blanchard, a devoted Catholic and nephew of Michele Des Maris, donated a large amount and helped raise more money for a pipe organ for the new church. It was known as the largest and most powerful organ west of Saint Louis and was built by George Kilgen & Sons, Inc.. It arrived by freight car, weighed 11 tons, and took a month to install. It has two manuals, 25 stops, and almost 1,600 pipes. To announce its presence the church held a large concert on October 22, 1885. In 2007 the organ was restored and another big concert celebrated its revival.

The organ in Our Lady of Sorrows church in Las Vegas, New Mexico.

The building at 1807 West Plaza is adobe. It may be the former location of the Raynolds brothers' bank. John Veeder had the building restored in 1932 and donated it to the newly organized Las Vegas Historical Society. It has had other uses since then.

John DeWitt Veeder became a leading Las Vegas attorney. He arrived from the east in 1882. His brother, Elmo arrived eight years later, and the two entered into a law partnership. The Veeders lived on the second floor of their first building, 1815 West Plaza. The second Veeder building at 1809-1813 West Plaza, built in 1895, is the only panel brick building on the Plaza. It is a two story, three bay structure with the designing feature of brick work within the panels along the parapet. Later they built a carriage house to the right.

Nestled in the middle of this structure, at 1811, is the site of Sheriff Longmire's office of the popular television series. Much of the first five seasons during 2011–2016 were filmed here.

Plaza Hotel and Ilfeld Building, early 1900s.
Courtesy Citizens Committee for Historic Preservation.

On the northwest corner of Plaza and Hot Springs Boulevard is the Plaza Hotel built in 1881. After the railroad came in 1879 the community realized the great need of a new hotel to provide for visitors arriving on the trains. Benigno Romero led the charge to form the Plaza Hotel Company. The hotel became known as one of the finest hotels in the west. Late 19th century and early 20th century Las Vegas became known as a place to come to heal tuberculosis. People from all over the country arrived and many stayed in the Plaza Hotel, in good weather their chairs lined in front of the hotel. The tuberculosis patients formed an informal *lungers* club. In 1913, while filming some of his early movies, Romain Fielding located his staff headquarters there.

As the economy of Las Vegas declined so did the hotel, but in 1982–1983 a partnership, The Plaza Associates, meticulously restored the building. During the restoration a stranger walked into the building and told the owners, "I think I have something you may want. I found this banister railing in my barn." Indeed, it was the banister railing for one of the main staircases into the lobby. The hotel has now expanded into the Ilfeld building next door. In 2014 Allan Affeld purchased the hotel and it remains a mainstay on the Plaza and in all of Las Vegas.

Charles Ilfeld migrated from Germany to New Mexico in 1865. His route included stops in Santa Fe, Taos, and in 1867, Las Vegas. He established a small business on the Plaza which grew to become one of the largest in the territory. He and his partner Adolf Letcher began by suppling hay and grain to army forts and a stagecoach line. They also contracted with the Santa Fe Railway and the Mexican Central Railroad for cutting railroad ties. Much of the lumber for the ties was cut in the Rociada area about 30 miles northwest of Las Vegas. About 1875 Charles bought out his partner. In 1882 he built the first part of this building at 224 North Plaza. Note the seam between the first three rows of windows and the latter five rows of windows. The second part of the building was added in 1890. One former employee enjoyed telling people, "Liquor in the basement, coffins on the top floor and everything in-between." Charles was guided by an age-old Spanish proverb: *"Cuando te compran, Vende!* When they are buying, sell!" He sold tools for farmers and ranchers, groceries, women's fine hats and dress making materials, furniture and most anything else that was needed.

Ilfeld then began concentrating his business on wool. He worked with sheep ranchers on the *partido* or sharecropping system and by 1904 the company had an interest in 33,000 sheep. He was very generous to community ventures, to all of his customers, even buying some of their debts and allowing them extended time to pay. However, he was quite frugal with his employees and had a hard time keeping them. He would pay no more than the market price of $15 to $20 a month while sheep shearers earned $2.00 per day. The average work week was 12 hours or more a day, with some time off on Sundays. In 1876 Las Vegas abolished Sunday hours. By 1883 wages increased to $33 a month and as labor demanded, continued to gradually increase.

Rodney Schoonmaker was Ilfeld's bookkeeper. When hired in 1884 the single-entry system appalled him. His suggestion for a double entry system was not initially accepted, so for a few months, until it was approved, he kept two sets of books.

Schoonmaker was an outstanding and very generous man. One story about him revealed that he sold his own land to keep another young man from going bankrupt, because he thought it was disrespectful to back out of one's debts. The holder of those debts gave Schoonmaker the lifetime use of the ranch. Later, when he was over 80 years old, and hospitalized he kept a file of more than a hundred 3x5 inch cards by his bed. Every day he wrote to someone in the service in World War II. He probably knew most of them personally. On a regular basis he took a dime's worth of candy to an abandoned friend at the State Hospital.

Max Nordhouse, a relative from Germany joined Charles in the company and they made three steps to protect the business: 1. Specializing in sheep and wool; 2. Fought to control the price by demand and; 3. Extended the mercantile credit system. The store closed in 1905 and the company moved to Albuquerque.

Max married and they had a son Robert. Robert married Virginia in 1935. Robert was involved with the development of the Sandia Ski area. A fun story about Nordhouses. We were on a vacation in 1984 and on a bus in Florida from the airport to the dock of a cruise ship. I struck up a conversation with my seat partner, who was from Rhode Island. When asked where I was from, I replied, "Northern New Mexico." "Where?" "A small town, probably you have never heard of, Las Vegas, New Mexico." She snapped back, "Have you ever heard of the Gallinas Canyon?" I was talking with Virginia Nordhouse, the daughter-in-law of Max Nordhouse. At that time the summer home in Gallinas was still owned by the Nordhouse or Ilfeld family. On board the ship we had a good conversation. More information on that in the Montezuma part of the tour.

Next to the large Ilfeld building at 220 North Plaza is a small red building. This was the law office of Louis Ilfeld, one of Charles' sons, and the lawyer for the firm. In the latter part of the 20th century the building was restored and for many years the home of the charming Los Artesanos Book Store.

The low building next to the law office, the Dice apartments at 210-218 North Plaza, is the only building still in existence that predates 1846. When General Kearny and his troops marched through this area in 1846 he stood on top of this building and told the people assembled in the Plaza that they were now part of the United States. These people had seen the Spanish and Mexican flags fly over the land so their attitude at first was, "So we fly another flag." Later there was rebellion centering more in the Taos and Mora areas where Governor Charles Bent and others were killed. In 1852 Frank Kihlberg purchased the building and lived there for 30 years. He had his Santa Fe Trail business next door to his residence.

Little is known about the building at 204-208 North Plaza, except being built in 1903 and recorded with the name Montoya Building. Next is the Gonzales Building at 200-202 North Gonzales, built in 1887 perhaps it belonged to Jesus Gonzales. He built a grist mill on the arroyo close to the end of the street near South Pacific. The street then became known as Gonzales Street.

At 1816 East Plaza Hilario and his brother Benjamin Romero opened a mercantile business. However, the store was known only as H. Romero and Brother. Hilario had been a freighter on the Santa Fe Trail and later as a brave sheriff for two years.

In the 1980s a young single mother, Carla Gomez, who had become an accomplished weaver started a weaving teaching/business in an abandoned school and later moved into 1816 East Plaza. She taught weaving, particularly to people struggling to support families, provided a venue to sell their products and helped them connect to other markets outside Las Vegas. That business, Tapate de Lana, moved to Mora, New Mexico. Next for many years, a popular coffee/lunch shop, Travelers Café offered the community tasty refreshments and meeting space.

1810 East Plaza may be a remodeling of the Des Marais' house. Michele Des Marais may have been the first French-Canadian to settle in Las Vegas. He came to New Mexico in 1837 and to Las Vegas in 1852. The Des Maraises became an established and prominent merchant family. Many of Michele's family and friends followed him to the area. Now for several years the building has been the Parish Hall for Our Lady of Sorrows Church.

As early as 1913 Romaine Fielding was the first to recognize what Las Vegas offers for the movie industry. The climate with over 300 days of sunshine per year, yet with four distinct seasons, geography with nearby mountains, plains and forests, plus a diversified variety of architecture provides unique location for dozens of movies and television films. Many are filmed here around the Plaza, but also throughout the town. A few movies and tv productions you may recognize are: *Red Dawn, No Country for Old Men, All the Pretty Horses, Wyatt Earp, Longmire, Roswell,* and many more.

Now continue the tour. Go around the Plaza and just before Bridge Street turn right on South Gonzales between the West Las Vegas School Administration building and the Navajo Textile building. Just past the intersection of South Gonzales and Moreno pull over and stop.

3
EL DISTRITO DE LAS ESCUELAS
(THE DISTRICT OF THE SCHOOLS)

There are six historical districts in Las Vegas. Although many of the buildings in El Distrito de Las Escuelas are gone it still plays an important part in the history of the community. South Gonzales Street was a quiet pleasant residential street with houses on both sides. Several of the well-to-do merchants had homes here. In contrast to the busy South Pacific street, houses on South Gonzales face the street with yards and perhaps flowers contributing to a pleasant neighborhood effect. Many of the houses with their thick adobe walls and historical trim were built prior to 1880 and are still standing.

Charles Ilfeld and family lived on the right side of South Gonzales near the corner. The home was not a mansion, but large and tastefully decorated. The gardens were beautiful, spacious and gracious. All that is left are the memories.

Before 1869 not much attention was given to education. The more affluent families may have engaged tutors or sent their sons away to school. In 1874 there were only 128 public schools in the whole Territory. Bishop Lamy came to New Mexico in 1851 and believed that the interests of the Catholic Church could best be served by a vigorous education program. He persuaded the sisters of Loretto to come to New Mexico. They first opened schools in Santa Fe and Albuquerque. In 1869 they opened a day and boarding school in Las Vegas on the southeast corner of Moreno and South Gonzales.

Sisters of Loretto School on South Gonzales.
Courtesy Citizens Committee for Historic Preservation.

When they arrived, there was no building for them. Rumaldo Baca lent them a small house on West National across the street from the new Our Lady of Sorrows Church. At night the three sisters slept on pallets on the floor and during the day taught the three R's to their 75 students. Contributions started arriving and in 1876 construction began on a two-story building on the east side of South Gonzales near the Plaza. Due to a fire in the first school they needed to move to the new building before it was completed. In 1888 they had 180 students. In 1912 they added a new school in East Las Vegas. In 1963 the South Gonzales school was abandoned and then burned in 1970.

Students of Sisters of Loretto School.
Courtesy Citizens Committee for Historic Preservation.

38

Continue your tour on South Gonzales.

On your left take note of the current West Las Vegas High School and Middle School complex. Past these schools still on the left between the *Acequia Madre* (the main irrigation ditch) and the river the Jesuits built a new school and called it the Las Vegas College. The college enrollment grew to 164 students. In 1881 the San Miguel County Commissioners designated the College to serve as the public school for that precinct and allocated funds. (We will learn about their first school when we turn onto South Pacific.)

The Jesuits were very popular in Las Vegas. Townspeople started going to them for confession and attending mass at their chapel. Soon they began giving to the Jesuits instead of the local church, which was struggling to complete its construction. The dissension led the Jesuits to move to Colorado and establish the Regis College in Denver. For a while a small contingent of Jesuits remained in Las Vegas to continue the publication of the Catholic magazine, *La Revista Catolica.*

The Christian Brothers arrived in 1888 and used the Las Vegas College as well as constructing their building on Valencia Street. They offered classes for 130 students grades 1-12 including several boarders.

Continue to the intersection of South Gonzales and South Pacific Streets.

Look to your left at the site of J. Gonzales' grist mill.

4
SOUTH PACIFIC AREA

South Pacific was the main route wagon trains used to continue their trip to Santa Fe and on south. The first railroad to obtain a charter was the New Mexico and Southern Pacific Railroad. In anticipation of the railroad using this route people began calling the street Southern Pacific, later shortened to South Pacific. Then the Atchison, Topeka, and Santa Fe Railroad obtained the charter and the route chosen was a mile away, but the title for this street stuck for all these years.

Turn right onto South Pacific.

On your left is a park, slightly raised above the street. For many years this was the site of the South Pacific Public School.

On the northwest corner of Valley Street and South Pacific streets is the one-time home of Pat Garrett, the sheriff who arrested Billy the Kid. His daughter, Elizabeth, composed the New Mexico state song which was officially adopted in 1916.

In response to this busy road the houses on the right side put "their backs" to the street. The long low strip of homes built close to the street and had their yards and private areas facing the other direction.

At the upcoming curve turn left onto Socorro Street and again left on Chavez Street.

As you make these turns note the building in the triangle on your left. This adobe quadrangle structure was the first location of the Jesuit School.

Manual Romero and Francisco Lopez had houses here and lent them to the Jesuits for their school. The Romero house, built around a pleasant grassy area, was called the *La Casa Redonda*. The school opened in that building. It may also have been used as the governor's home, when Las Vegas served briefly as the territorial capital.

Stop for a moment on Chavez Street and look to your right at the Presbyterian Mission.

In 1869 the Presbyterian school was started in a private home by the Reverend John Annin. He and Jose Perea, a close associate, bought a house from George Chavez on South Chavez Street. They opened a boarding school. In 1870 they proceeded to build a combination church and school. It took about two years to complete. Strong competition from the Catholic community created many ups and downs for the Presbyterians, but churches in the east were looking for new missions to support and kept sending money. In the beginning to avert skepticism Annin and Perea called the school the San Miguel County Literacy Association. The church congregation remained small, much to the chagrin of a visiting mission developer, but by 1888 they had close to 180 students in the school. In 1896 they moved the school to Albuquerque where it is still in operation as the Menaul School.

Jose Ynez Perea was a very well educated, resourceful man and became the first native New Mexican to be ordained in the Presbyterian Church.

Now Make a U turn at Blanchard or turn right and go around the block to return to South Pacific and turn left.

Before reaching South Pacific look to your right and see *La Casa Redonda*.

Turn left and proceed on South Pacific.

Turn right at the corner of South Pacific and Moreno and pull over and stop for a moment.

The empty lot at the southeastern corner of Moreno and South Pacific is the former location of the Gazette newspaper. In the early 1870s, the *Gazette* was a prominent morning newspaper of West Las Vegas. In 1874 J.K. Koogler bought it. In 1879 the first train arrived east of the town of Las Vegas bringing amongst many other things, another newspaper editor, L.J. Keithley who established an evening paper, the *Las Vegas Optic*. Very quickly a strong long-lasting adversarial relationship developed between the two. Perhaps more than anything else these two newspapers promoted the separation of the east and west communities.

Mid-block on the right was the home of Vicente Silva. Across the street from the home was the back door of his bar known as either Victory Bar or Imperial Bar.

> **Go to the corner, make a U turn, go back to the corner of South Pacific, turn right, go half way around the Plaza and continue north on North Gonzales.**

5
ENROUTE TO MONTEZUMA

Continue on North Gonzales about two blocks and pull over and stop for a moment.

Watch for house number 2008. The front door of the house faces south to a large front yard. Read about the Jack Johnson versus Jim Flynn Heavy Weight Champion Fight.

In 1912 Jack Curley a nationally known fight promoter and Charles O'Malley, who lived in Las Vegas was a former major league baseball player, served as a scout for the Saint Louis Browns, and joined forces to bring a world championship boxing match to Las Vegas, New Mexico. Jack Johnson a heavyweight champion and Jim Flynn a contender agreed to a July 4, 1912 fight.

Flynn trained at the Montezuma Hotel gym and Jackson trained at the residence, 2008 North Gonzales. Staff set up plank seats in the yard of Johnson's training area and people paid ten cents a person to come and watch him work out sparring against partners.

Group gathered for the 1912 Johnson/Flynn Heavy Weight
National Championship Fight.
Jack Johnson is in the center.
Courtesy Citizens Committee for Historic Preservation.

All was coming into place with special trains scheduled for the event, the stadium being built east of the old Saint Anthony's Sanitarium (now New Mexico Behavior Health Institute) and advance ticket sales going well. Then a series of disasters ensued.

O'Malley and the stadium contractor had serious differences about the stadium and a late snowstorm hampered the construction. Some New Mexico ministers and a few legislators started a campaign against boxing matches in the territory. Laguna Native Americans agreed, because the territory would not allow them to schedule fights. The Santa Fe railroad learned of the unrest and cancelled some of the trains. Ticket sales slowed. Governor McDonald then issued a proclamation that "No pugilistic events would be held during my term." At the last minute he recanted, the fight took place and Jack Johnson handily won the fight, but it became known as boxing's greatest fiasco.

Continue north about one and a half blocks turn left on the one-way Bernallio Street. Continue to Hot Springs Boulevard and turn left. Go one block and pull over and stop at a large two-story home with a balcony across the front.

44

Benigno Romero's house is located here at 2003 Hot Springs Boulevard. His father, Miguel, had five sons and several daughters, but in those times it was often only the sons' work that was documented. The community held the Romero brothers in special regard, because they were very generous with their wealth both to individuals and special causes.

Benigno was a leader in the business community, but perhaps best known for his concern of the mentally ill. He cared for mentally ill in his home. In 1891 he was instrumental in convincing the territorial legislature to build a mental health hospital in Las Vegas.

> **Continue on Hot Springs Boulevard turn left into the parking lot make a "U" turn and turn right (north) on Hot Springs Boulevard.**
>
> **Proceed north slowly on Hot Springs Boulevard.**

On the west side of the street at 2315 Hot Springs Boulevard, now the site the Gonzales Funeral and Cremations, was the home of Jefferson Raynolds. Jefferson and his brother Joshua founded Central Bank, the oldest bank in Las Vegas (later to become the First National Bank).

At 2323 Hot Springs Boulevard is the former home of Charles A. Spiess, a respected lawyer in Las Vegas. In 1910 he served as the chairman of a committee to adopt a constitution for New Mexico and to prepare for admittance to the United States. He also helped organize an appropriate Land Grant Board and other policies for the good of the community.

> **Continue north on Hot Springs Boulevard for about a five to six mile trip toward Montezuma, with stops in between.**
>
> **About a half mile north from Mills on your left pull into the parking lot of Meadows Long Term Care Facility and park for a few minutes to read about the State Hospital.**

Meadows has been associated with the State Hospital for years. It reorganized and this new building was completed in 2012. A third phase is to be completed in mid to late 2021.

In great part due to the efforts of Benigno Romero, in 1889 the territorial legislature took steps to establish an asylum in Las Vegas. It took constant pressure to keep the project moving. In 1892 a three-story building was ready, but it did not have operating funds until 1893. In 1895 forty-five patients received care and a new wing was needed to handle the demand.

First New Mexico Mental Hospital.
Courtesy Citizens Committee for Historic Preservation.

The hospital has gone by different names: The Insane Asylum, The State Hospital, Behavior Health Center and most recently the Las Vegas Medical Center. It continues to serve the state and now employs between 500 and 700 hundred people and is a major employer of the community.

Return to Hot Springs Boulevard. Turn left.

On your left are the foot hills of the Sangre de Cristo Mountain Range. A legend tells us that during the bloody Pueblo Indian Revolt of 1680 a priest was praying for a sign that God was with him and then the mountains turned red. He named the mountains Sangre de Cristo (blood of Christ). The highest peak in New Mexico is about 13,000 feet and the range is home to five ski areas. Las Vegas depends in part on the seasonal runoff for its water supply.

Continue north about one mile on Hot Springs Boulevard turn left and start to head up the hill, and part way up turn left again to Luna Community College.

On the top of the *creston* (hill) is a great view of Las Vegas and surrounding area.

Park where it is convenient and read about this area on the marker.

6
LUNA COMMUNITY COLLEGE AND MORE

Step out of your car and look east. On the horizon you may see a small cluster of buildings. This is the Las Vegas Airport. Aviation started in this area as early as 1927, although at an airstrip a few miles away. In 1933 sporadic airmail began. By 1937 regular airmail and passenger flights served Las Vegas until 1951. In 1940 Las Vegas was designated as Flight Service Station to give pilots official weather and other information. During this time Las Vegas was fortunate to have two airlines flying to the community: Continental and Pioneer.

If one individual was to be singled out as to having contributed the most to aviation in the Las Vegas area it would by J. Lloyd Bible. He arrived in Las Vegas in 1927 as a baker for the Fred Harvey Hotel. About 1929 he had a few flying lessons. He then bought a plane in Wyoming and flew it home alone. He had an unlicensed plane so he reasoned he didn't need a license to fly it! By 1931 he had his license and started giving lessons.

As World War II loomed closer the U. S. military was looking for qualified pilots with over 1000 hours flying time to become instructors. Lloyd Bible and two others became the first licensed instructors in New Mexico.

Naval Air Training Planes at Las Vegas, New Mexico Airport.
Courtesy Citizens Committee for Historic Preservation.

In 1942 New Mexico Highlands University and the Las Vegas Airport became a War Training Service where pilots were trained for the military. The U. S. government furnished 40 small planes. The University taught the ground school information and Lloyd Bible was responsible for the flight training. Later small private planes were conscripted. At first there were eight students, but then the program grew to approximately 125. The program was then called the Navy Pilot Training and Bible enlisted other instructors to help him.

At the end of the program Bible had the opportunity to buy some of the planes. He stayed in Las Vegas and for many years operated a charter service and continued to give flying lessons until about 1980.

In the early 1900s Company A of the National Guard made their first encampment in Las Vegas on 8th Street north of Saint Anthony's Sanitarium's, (now New Mexico Behavior Health Institute). For years off and on summer encampments took place there.

In the early 1920s the Las Vegas Chamber of Commerce underwrote the purchase of 668 acres for a more permanent National Guard Camp in the general location of the current Luna Community College. The area was soon named Camp Maximiliano Luna in honor of an officer who served with F Company of Teddy Roosevelt Rough Riders and later died while in the service in the Philippines. In 1924 the first buildings were erected.

King's Stadium. Courtesy Citizens Committee for Historic Preservation.

Summer encampments could hold as many as 3,500 men and greatly helped the local economy. As part of the military installation in 1935 a large stadium was constructed on the back side of the property. Numerous horse shows and community activities were held here.

During World War II the site became home to the Army Air Force Ferry Command. Shortly after the war Camp Luna was dismantled and about one third of the buildings were destroyed. September 1, 1959 the Guard reorganized.

Camp Luna Army Air Force Ferry Command.
Courtesy Citizens Committee for Historic Preservation.

Luna Vocational Technical Institute opened its first classes in the fall of 1970 with only 45 students, but enrollment grew quickly. In the year 2000 it became Luna Community College with majors in several different fields and vocational career training in a few areas. In the fall of 2019 enrollment was 1043. It has filled an important educational niche in Northeastern New Mexico with vocational training, Registered Nurse and associate degrees, GED certificates and more.

In 1884 on top of the same hill, but across the road from the National Guard Complex the Atchison, Topeka, Santa Fe Railroad Company built an eleven room hospital for its employees. During the first six months of operation the company doctor treated 108 patients. Later a hospital was built in Albuquerque and this hospital was withdrawn from service in 1922. The property was then sold several different times.

Now come back down the hill, turn left onto Hot Springs Boulevard and continue north.

7
HOT SPRINGS BRANCH RAILROAD

In 1892 about a half mile east of Hot Springs Boulevard roughly following the Gallinas River a spur railroad line was built from Las Vegas to Montezuma. Starting at 9:00 a.m. trains departed Las Vegas every two hours for a thirty-minute ride to Montezuma. On arrival, passengers disembarked at the depot on the south side of the river. Carriages would come to the north side, passengers would walk across the bridge and then be taken to the hotel. This spur line was also a key part of ice business and proved to be very helpful for firemen (which turned out to be important) to make a fast trip to Montezuma.

As you drive on Hot Springs Boulevard, the road will make a left turn and you can see the Montezuma Post Office on your right.

> **You may choose to go right onto the grounds of the United World College. Stop at the security gate and ask for permission to walk around. Or can turn left and watch for the hot springs.**

Montezuma

The large building you see is fondly referred to as the Castle. It is now part of the United World College of the American West. Nearby there are hot springs. A legend says that various Native American tribes used the springs and felt they were sacred grounds and no violence could be committed there. If one tribe was using the springs the other would wait its turn.

When the Southwest was claimed by other countries, Spain, Mexico, and the United States those countries assumed ownership of the hot springs area. J & A Donaldson contacted the *alcalde* (mayor) of West Las Vegas and acquired a grant for the hot springs from the Our Lady of Sorrows Land Grant. They built a small bathhouse. Next the Army purchased it and constructed a long, low adobe building to house wounded and ill soldiers from nearby Fort Union. In 1864 the Army sold the property to an entrepreneur who converted the hospital to a hotel, The Adobe. One of its notorious guests was Jesse James.

When the railroad came to Las Vegas in 1879, a new company formed, the Las Vegas Hot Springs Company, with the railroad as the controlling shareholder. They purchased the property and built a two story bathhouse with 14 bathing rooms. The building included a pharmacy and a doctor's residence on the second floor. Fires presented major problems. On April 12, 1880 the bath house burned to the ground.

An anecdote involves Dr. Oliver, the resident physician and his wife. During the night Dr. Oliver awakened to something strange and stepped out of the apartment. He discovered the fire, ran back to the apartment, scooped up his sleeping wife and threw her out the window! She survived the twenty-foot fall, but not sure how well she slept after that! Someone came with a ladder to help her husband down.

In 1880 building continued with a three story seventy-five room stone hotel. To celebrate the opening of the hotel, guests at the ball danced all night. North of the hot springs this building still stands and is used by the United World College.

In 1882 the company made plans for a new, frame 240 room hotel on the north central part of the now playing field of the United World College. The hotel included a dining hall, bowling alleys, a billiards room all lit with gas lights. Just in time for its opening the railroad spur line was completed. The depot was located near the power plant on the south side of the property. Carriages would meet guests for the short ride to the hotel.

Gas for the lights was processed in the basement of the hotel. When passing to the lights outside the gas could condense on the pipes, but would then flow into special designed traps. Workmen were scheduled to regularly empty these traps. On the day of this fire at one p.m. workmen assigned to clean the traps, had gone to the basement with spirt lamps, and had just started when they were called to fix a stove. When they returned there was a small explosion and quickly an inferno.

The railroad provided an extra engine and flat car to transport fire equipment, firemen, and volunteers to fight the fire. It took only about twenty minutes for the fire train to arrive, but the firemen realized it was too late to save the hotel as already the heat was extreme and the skeleton of the building was visible. Complicating the fire was the hotel building material of seasoned pine, which burns very fast, no "party walls" (safety walls between sections) and perhaps frozen hydrants. Since the fire was at mid-day and the manager immediately realized saving the hotel was hopeless, he efficiently evacuated the hotel. Miraculously there were no deaths.

Immediately the company began construction on a new hotel making it as fireproof as possible. They built on the hill above the former hotel, with stone as a major building material. The reservoir was increased to hold six million gallons of water at 60 pounds of pressure per inch on the upper floors. Fire plugs and hoses were placed in every hall. All rooms were equipped with mercurial fire alarms and all were connected to a general alarm in the clerk's office. The hotel was heated with steam radiators and hot air furnaces and lit with electricity.

Montezuma Hotel early 1880s.
Courtesy Citizens Committee for Historic Preservation.

The new hotel boasted marble bathroom fixtures, two bowling alleys, several billiard rooms and the first elevator in the area. Nonetheless, only a few months after the hotel opened a fire alarm sounded at 10:30 p.m. The fire started in the attic and hotel employees tried to extinguish the flames, but they had not been trained, got tangled in the hoses and in each others' way. The halls or the hoses had not been measured and the hoses were too short. Fire departments arrived quickly: Company One in two minutes less than the previous fire and E. Romero shortly after. The fire was contained by 2:30 a.m. but the hotel had been destroyed down to the stone level.

In August 1886 the third Montezuma hotel opened, rebuilt on the remaining stone walls. There was talk of renaming it the Phoenix for the Egyptian legend that it rose from its ashes and restored itself to is youthful state, but the Montezuma name stayed in popular usage.

Economic hard times lay ahead for the hotel, but it had had a remarkable history. Eminent people from other countries, President Grant and other prominent guests from the U.S. stayed at the hotel. One large convention brought 1,000 people on two special trains to the hotel. But in 1886, recruiting visitors was more difficult, perhaps because of the fires, or that the railroad was now promoting resorts farther west. In 1893 there was a major nationwide railroad strike and visitation dropped drastically. In

1903 the Las Vegas Hot Springs Company gave the property to the YMCA drawing to a close the hotel era.

In 1920 the YMCA turned the property over to the Southern Baptist Convention for use as a college. The Great Depression was approaching and the college had financial difficulties. A story circulated about two girls from the east coming to attend the college. They arrived by train in Las Vegas, hired a ride to Montezuma, and were dropped off at a rather dark old hotel. They knocked on the door and someone opened it a crack and the girls said they were here to enroll in classes. "The college is closed." And the door also closed. Somehow they got back to Las Vegas, and then got jobs as Harvey girls at the Casteneda Hotel.

The next page of the history of the hotel began in 1937 with the return of the Jesuits. The property was purchased by the Catholic Church to be used as a Jesuit seminary for young Mexicans. In Mexico for much of the last century the church and state were estranged and there was a need for seminaries outside of the country. For 35 years the seminary here educated over 2,200 students and ordained 1,300 priests. The community and the seminary had a close relationship. The seminary closed in 1970 and a period of about ten years of vacancy and vandalism ensued.

Perhaps as the early as 1950s Lord Mountbattten, Earl of Burma (great uncle of Prince Charles) and Kurt Hahn of Outward Bound were visiting about the world situation, the status of education for young people and how the two intertwined. They agreed that to make effective change in the world any plan had to start with the young people. Lord Mountbatten proposed strong education. Kurt Hahn agreed and inserted that the plan must include outdoor activities. The idea was born to establish a series of schools across the world using the International Baccalaureate curriculum and include training in outdoor skills. Schools should be located close to mountains or the sea to provide for rescue training in those areas. There would be only one such school per country and the enrollment would reflect a strong international cross section. The first school opened in 1962 in Wales.

Shortly before Lord Mountbatten's untimely death, Armand Hammer became interested in the project and wanted one of these schools in the United States. He would cover the initial investment. His search crew found over 100 sites for Hammer to peruse. Students are selected on their abilities to contribute to the good of the cause not their ability to pay. In choosing a site the selection committee did not want a place that would be offensive to students from third world countries. Perhaps the poverty of San Miguel County was an advantage in this situation! The Armand Hammer United World College opened in the fall of 1982. HRH Prince Charles, then president of the United World College movement, attended the opening.

United World College committees situated worldwide seek nominations and applications from qualified students. The two year UWC schools select two students per year from countries across the world. The Armand Hammer United World College is a boarding school with about 230 students representing 70-80 countries at any time. Classes are taught in English with English as a Second Language course being necessary for many students. In the United States it is acknowledged as a senior year of high school and freshman year of college school.

There is a "Getaway" program at the UWC-US where families in the community may apply to "adopt" a student to visit on week-ends, holidays, etc. Many lifelong friendships are formed. One student from Lesotho slowly revealed his background to his Getaway family. He got up at four in the morning and ran 12 miles to school. His mother swept their dirt floor and the yard, prepared meals, cared for the animals, and other household tasks. His father met with the men in the village. The student arrived at the Albuquerque airport with little or no English, wearing perhaps his first pair of shoes, saying his name and the name of the school. This intelligent, brave young man from Lesotho was one of the many who accepted the challenge and honor of attending the UWC. A prince from Greece, wealthy student from Hollywood, student from rural North Dakota, and others are all treated the same, all are to have about the same amount of spending money per month, no cars and no student may drive. The majority of the students are on full scholarships.

At one time the *Las Vegas Optic* reported that a student from Somaliland a region of Somalia not recognized by any other country, and attending the now known United World College of the American West, had received a full scholarship to MIT. He was one of 11 children born into a nomadic family with no schools close by. His grandmother offered to take him into her home in a village where there was a school. As he excelled and through various channels was found by the UWC system and received a full scholarship. It is an amazing program.

The curriculum is challenging as well as the intense effort to help students learn about and respect other cultures. In 2010 U.S. Center for Citizen Diplomacy ranked UWC-USA a "Top Ten Program".

If you have gone to the United World College, return to post office turn right onto the highway and past the hot springs. If you went to the hot springs first, now continue west to a slight fork in the road. Take the left fork into a large dirt parking area. Park looking at the pond. <u>Do not go up the hill</u>.

8
ICE PONDS

In the 1880s ice was in high demand. The Agua Pura Company incorporated in 1880. Part of the business plan included making ice to help meet this demand. The company built nine dams on the Gallinas River and for years each winter hired about 300 men or more, cutting ice, storing it in ice houses, packing it with straw and loading railroad cars. In 1909 the estimated harvest was 60,000 tons. In 1910 the Aqua Pura Company had a contract to provide ice to California, Arizona as well as southern New Mexico using all 2,500 railroad carloads and all the ice the ponds could produce. Due to the coming of refrigeration, the ice company closed in the early 1930s.

The Agua Pura Company Railroad along the Gallinas River.
Courtesy Citizens Committee for Historic Preservation.

However, the pond closest to Montezuma provided years of ice skating entertainment. About three months each winter, after school and weekends the pond would be busy with skaters. Often the seminarians would clear the pond and for many years there was a little concession stand renting skates and selling hot chocolate. Then problems with the dam put an end to the skating.

Ice Skating on Pond near the Montezuma Hotel.
Courtesy Citizens Committee for Historic Preservation.

Up the Gallinas is a little community called Trout Springs. The Nordhouse family had a summer home there. Virginia Nordhouse recalled her first visit to New Mexico to meet her soon to be in-laws. She planned on coming into town dressed in jeans and boots as she expected Las Vegas to be a hick town. Her fiancé tentatively asked her to wear a skirt. They then went into town to the Herman Ilfeld home to meet more family. Charlotte, Herman's daughter was chicly dressed and Virginia noticed a picture of her being presented at court in England. Oh, maybe not a one-horse town!

At one time the family decided to participate in the Las Vegas Fourth of July parade. With much effort and help they restored an old carriage and got it down the Gallinas road and into Las Vegas. The whip holders were filled with beautiful wild flowers, the driver was dressed in top hat and gloves. The ladies had old finery including black parasols. After the parade the carriage and all arrived at one of the Ilfeld's for lunch and cocktails. Memories are made of things like this!

Sometimes there would be twenty to forty family members gathered at Trout Springs and always guests, some local and from a distance.

This completes your tour of West Las Vegas and Montezuma. You might now want to explore more on your own.

TO THE READER,

I hope you have enjoyed this tour. I first developed this tour as part of my Travels 'N' Trails Historical Tour Company, which disbanded many years ago. Now I have reorganized my notes for two volumes of self-guided tours of Las Vegas. This book is one of them.

BIBLIOGRAPHY

Books

Beck, Warren. *New Mexico, A History of Four Centuries*. Norman, OK: University of Oklahoma Press, 1962.

Cabeza de Baca, Manuel. *Vincente Silva and His Forty Bandits, His Crimes and Retributions*. Translated from the Spanish by Dolores Gutierrez Mills and Carment Cabeza de Baca Pace. Santa Fe, NM: Sunstone Press, 2022

Cather, Willa. *Death Comes to the Archbishop*. New York: Alford Knopf, 1966.

Calhoun, Milton. *Las Vegas, New Mexico, The Town That Wouldn't Gamble*. Las Vegas, NM: *Las Vegas Optic*, The Las Vegas Publishing Co., 1962.

Halverson, Patricia. *Development of Aviation in Northern New Mexico*. Masters Thesis, Las Vegas, NM: New Mexico Highlands University, 1979.

Huning, Franz and Browne, Lina Fergusson. *Trader on the Santa Fe Trail*. Albuquerque, NM: Calvin Horn Publisher, Inc, 1973.

Kessell, John. *Kiva, Cross, and Crown*. National Park Service, Washington, D.C.: U.S. Department of the Interior, 1979.

Lockwood, Theodore D. *Dreams and Promises, The Story of the Armand Hammer United World College*. Santa Fe, NM: Sunstone Press, 1997.

Magoffin, Susan. *Down the Santa Fe Trail and into Mexico: Diary of Susan Magoffin*. Lincoln, NB: University of Nebraska Press, 1982.

Naum, Milton. *Las Vegas and Uncle Joe*. Norman, OK: University of Oklahoma Press, 1964.

Perrigo, Lynn. *Gateway to Glorieta*. Santa Fe, NM: Sunstone Press, 2010.

Parish, William. *Charles Ilfeld Company*. Cambridge, MA: Harvard University Press,1961.

Romero, Edwina. *Las Vegas, New Mexico, 1835–1935*. Las Vegas, NM:

Friends of the City of Las Vegas Museum and Rough Riders Memorial Collection, 2018.

Romero, Edwina Portelle. *Footlights in the Foothills, Amateur Theatre of Los Vegas and Fort Union, New Mexico, 1871–1899.* Santa Fe, NM: Sunstone Press, 2011.

Rubio, H. *La Gente Del Oro Otra Lad.* Rociada, NM: Yucca Speedway Printers, 1980.

Rieniets, Thomas, *History of the Montezuma Hot Springs Hotels and Bathhouses, 1840–1937.* Masters Thesis, Las Vegas, NM: New Mexico Highlands University, 1966.

Stanley, F. *The Las Vegas, New Mexico Story.* Denver, CO: World Press, 1951.

Threinen, Ellen. *Architecture and Preservation in Las Vegas: The Study of Six Districts.* Las Vegas, NM: Funded by National Park Service Historical Grant, Project 35-76-00067.5, 1977.

Newspapers and Magazines

Albers, Gwen. "Somalian Student Gets Full Ride from MIT," *Las Vegas Optic,* February 24, 2021.

Bommersbach, Janna. "America's Most Famous Firehouse." *True West,* April, 2018.

Ivers, Louise, "The Pride of Las Vegas, New Mexico," *NMA,* March-April 1970.

Schackel, Sandra. "Charles Ilfeld, A Perspective on a New Mexico Mercantile Family," *El Palacio,*
Spring 1981.

Las Vegas Optic, April 13, 1880.

Las Vegas Optic, March 3, 1899.

(No author) "The Fire at Montezuma, Burns to the Ground." *Las Vegas Optic,* January 17, 1884.

(No author) "Social Work Degree to be Offered at HU," *Las Vegas Optic,* July 8, 1982.

Notes Given to Reporters on the Ground. "The Second Day." *Las Vegas Optic,* January 19, 1884.

Talbot, Steven. "Getting Lost in History in the Other Las Vegas," *The New York Times,* November 16, 2007.

Taichert, Daniel. "The Taichert Brothers and the American Dream." *New Mexico Jewish Historical Society, Legacy*, December, 2009.

Interviews and Lectures

Campbell, Rev. J. Randy. February, 2021.
Leach, Leah. Las Vegas, An Old Dignity Preserved.
Linder, Drs. Peter and Carol. Professors at New Mexico Highlands University, February, 2021.
Luna Community College, Public Relations office. February, 2021.
Nordhouse, Virginia. Rendezvous Bar on the ship Atlantic, in the Caribbean, 1984.
McKinnley, Jeanne. CCHP office, February, 2021.
Taichert, Milton. Taichert residence, Summer 1981.
Wilson, Chris. Las Vegas, New Mexico, May, 1984.

Scholarly Papers

Bennett, David, and John C. de Baca. *A Brief History of the Montezuma Hotels.*
Perrigo, Lynn I., *El Distrito de Las Escuelas,* New Mexico Highlands University, 1973.
Perrigo, Lynn I., *The Former Residence of Don Benigno Romero,* Las Vegas, New Mexico, 1976.

Other

Flyer from Our Lady of Sorrows Church 2007.
Perrigo, Lynn I. Audio tapes, Carnegie Library, Las Vegas, New Mexico.
The Aqua Pura Company of Las Vegas Certificate of Incorporation.

www.ingramcontent.com/pod-product-compliance
Lightning Source LLC
Chambersburg PA
CBHW022032080426
42733CB00007B/814